Aussie English for Beginners

Cartoons by David Pope

**NATIONAL
MUSEUM OF
AUSTRALIA**
C A N B E R R A

First published 2002 by
  National Museum of Australia
  GPO Box 1901
  CANBERRA ACT 2601
  Phone +61 2 6208 5000
  Fax +61 2 6208 5148
  Email information@nma.gov.au
  Website www.nma.gov.au

Reprinted 2003

National Library of Australia cataloguing-in-publication data:
  Pope, David.
  Aussie English for Beginners.

  ISBN 1 876944 06 4.

  1. English language — Australia — Caricatures and cartoons.
  2. English language — Australia — Dictionaries. I. Title.

  423.1

Designed and typeset by Roar Creative, Canberra
Printed by Elect Printing, Canberra

In so many ways, Australia is different from any other country, anywhere in the world. Nowhere else has kangaroos, dingos, tiger snakes and lamingtons. Nowhere else comes to a complete standstill for ten minutes one day a year to watch a horserace.

We're special ... and so is our language.

Australian English has, over time, developed a rich vocabulary that some would say reflects our dry wit and occasional wisdom. It also reflects our different cultures and origins. Many Aussie words are derived from Aboriginal languages, many are from old forms or usages of English, and some are from other countries. All have taken on distinctly Australian meanings. 'Noah', for example, might mean a Biblical figure to most people, to Aussies it's rhyming slang for shark.

We have successfully exported some of our words and phrases to other countries. Through events such as the Sydney Olympics, the whole world can now confidently say 'G'day mate' while they chuck a snag on the barbie, crack a tinnie or open a bottle of plonk.

Aussie English for Beginners explores the origins and meanings of just a few of our many common Australian words, with definitions provided by the Australian National Dictionary Centre and cartoons by David Pope. It is based on a display in the Nation: Symbols of Australia gallery of the National Museum of Australia.

And it's bonzer, mate!

Bilby

A small marsupial with soft blue-grey fur, pointed snout and long ears. It lives in the desert and digs a deep burrow, venturing out at night to hunt for insects, seeds and fruit. Recently, the **Easter bilby** has become a popular alternative to the **Easter bunny**. The word was borrowed from Yuwaalaraay, an Aboriginal language of northern New South Wales, and was first recorded in 1885.

Bludger

A person who does not do a fair share of work and who exploits the work of others. The word comes from the British slang word **bludger**, shortened from **bludgeoner**, a prostitute's pimp, so named because he carried a bludgeon, presumably to ensure payment. In Australia, **bludger** came to be applied to anyone who did not pull his or her weight.

Bonzer

Outstandingly good — 'they make a bonzer meat pie'. This is one of many Australian terms whose meaning is clear, but whose origins are doubtful. Possible origins include an alteration of the American **bonanza**, or the French word **bon** 'good', or from a British dialect **bouncer** meaning 'anything very large of its kind'.

Bullbar

A strong metal frame fitted to the front of a vehicle to protect it if it has a collision. In the bush a vehicle might hit stray cattle (thus the name **bullbar**) or a kangaroo (thus the alternative name **kangaroo bar** or **roo bar**). This Australian word, first recorded in 1967, has spread to other countries.

Bung

Broken, exhausted, out of action — 'the TV's bung'. It comes from bang meaning 'dead', which was first recorded in 1841 in the Yagara Aboriginal language of the Brisbane region. The word found its way into nineteenth-century Australian pidgin, where the phrase **to go bung** meant 'to die'. By the end of the nineteenth century, the present sense had developed.

Bunyip

This people-eating monster of Aboriginal legend has been keenly adopted by non-Aboriginal artists and writers. Descriptions of it vary greatly: some give it a frightful human head and an animal body; some emphasise its threat to humans and its loud booming at night. It is said to inhabit inland rivers, swamps and billabongs. The word comes from the Aboriginal Wergaia language of western Victoria, and was first recorded in 1845.

The bush

The **bush** means country more or less covered with forest or scrub. This sense appears earliest in South Africa and America, and is from the Dutch **bosch** 'woodland'. But the phrase **the bush** has special meaning in Australia. It refers to any area outside the major cities, and symbolises the views and experiences of those in the bush compared to city dwellers. It was first recorded in 1790.

Chook

A domestic fowl. **Chook** comes from British dialect **chuck** or **chucky** 'chicken', a word imitating a hen's cluck. Australians use 'chicken' to mean 'the meat of the bird' or 'a baby fowl'. **Chook** is the common term for the live bird, **old chook** usually refers to a fussy or silly older woman. It was first recorded as **chuckey** in 1855.

Compo

Payment, made under a workers' compensation scheme, for injury or illness suffered in the course of work. The word was first recorded in 1941. The addition of the **-o** ending to abbreviated words is common in colloquial Australian English. For example: **smoko** 'a tea or smoking break'; **garbo** 'garbage collector'; **arvo** 'afternoon'; and **rego** 'motor vehicle registration'.

Croweaters

A nickname for South Australians, who were
popularly mocked in the nineteenth century as
eating crows in times of hardship. Similarly,
Queenslanders are **bananabenders** (they put
the bends in bananas), and Queenslanders
call people 'south of the border' **Mexicans**.
Tasmanians are **Apple Islanders**, Western
Australians are **sandgropers**, and Northern
Territorians are **Top Enders**.

Dag

A person who is unkempt, unfashionable or lacking in social skills. The word **dag** also means a lump of matted wool and dung hanging from a sheep's rear. This sense probably led to the meaning 'unkempt', and then to the broader meanings 'unfashionable' and 'socially unacceptable'. It was first recorded in 1891.

Dinkum

Dinky-di Aussies use this word to mean 'genuine, honest, true'. It comes from the British Midlands term **dinkum**, meaning 'a fair share of work'. First recorded in 1888, it was not borrowed from the Chinese words *ding kam* meaning 'top gold', as is often believed. And that's **fair dinkum**.

Donkey vote

Australia is one of few nations in the world where voting is compulsory. Voters are expected to rank each candidate in order of preference. When voters simply number the candidates in the order they appear on the ballot paper, without weighing their merits, they are casting a **donkey vote** — a vote worthy of a donkey.

Don't come the raw prawn with me!

This colourful Australian phrase, first recorded in the 1940s, refers to a story that is hard to believe. In polite language, 'don't try to deceive me!', 'don't try to make a fool of me!'.

Dreamtime

In Aboriginal belief, the events and time when spirit ancestors shaped the physical, spiritual and moral worlds. The **Dreamtime**, or **Dreaming**, continues as a powerful influence in the lives of Aboriginal people today. **Dreamtime**, first recorded in 1896, is a translation of *altyerre* 'dream' and *-nge* 'in', 'out of' in the Northern Territory Aboriginal language Arrernte.

Drop bear

A modern-day mythical animal similar in appearance to a koala, but about 1.5 metres in height, with very sharp claws and teeth. They are said to eat other animals, and to have a taste for humans. **Drop bears** lurk in trees, and drop down on their unsuspecting victims, especially overseas tourists.

Economic rationalism

An approach to economic management that allows market forces, such as supply and demand, to direct the economy. This approach typically adopts privatisation, deregulation, 'user pays' and low public spending. Most Australians are surprised to discover that this is an Australian term.

Fairy bread

Slices of white bread cut into triangles, buttered and sprinkled with tiny, coloured sugar balls called 'hundreds and thousands'. **Fairy bread** is frequently served at children's parties in Australia. The name possibly comes from the poem 'Fairy Bread' in Robert Louis Stevenson's *A Child's Garden of Verses*, published in 1885.

Fossick

To search for gold. In the Cornish dialect, **fossick** means 'to obtain by asking, to ferret out'. Cornish miners probably brought the term here in the 1850s and used it to describe their search for gold. The word widened in meaning and can now refer to searching or rummaging for anything — 'fossicking in the drawer for a pen'.

Furphy

An untrue rumour, an absurd story. The firm J Furphy & Sons, of Shepparton in Victoria, made water carts on which the name Furphy appeared in large letters. In Egypt during the First World War, the drivers of these carts often carried rumours and gossip into the camps. Any false rumour therefore came to be called a **furphy**.

G'day

'Good day', a friendly greeting used at any hour. The shortened version was first recorded in 1928. Some claim that this kind of abbreviation is typical of Australian speech. In its extreme form, the running together of syllables is called **Strine**, an alleged Australian pronunciation of 'Australian'. 'Air conditioner' is **eggnishner** in Strine.

Jackeroo

In the 1840s, **jackeroo** referred to a white man living outside settled areas. By the 1870s, it had acquired its current meaning of a young man working on a cattle or sheep station to acquire farm-management skills. There is no evidence that it comes from an Indigenous language, but is possibly from **jack** 'labourer' as in 'lumberjack', and modelled on the **-aroo** ending of **kangaroo**. **Jillaroo** appeared during the Second World War when women took on many of the jobs once reserved for men.

Koori

An Aboriginal person, usually from south-eastern Australia. First recorded in 1834, **Koori** comes from the term for 'Aboriginal man or person' in the language of the Awabakal Aboriginal people of eastern New South Wales, and in neighbouring languages. It is now widely used throughout the south-eastern states. Different words for 'Aboriginal person' are used in other parts of Australia, such as **Murri**, **Nyungar**, **Palawa**, and **Yolngu**.

Larrikin

A person who thumbs his, and sometimes her, nose at social conventions and authority. The word, related to 'lark' as in 'lark about', came from the British dialects of Warwickshire and Worcestershire, and was first recorded in 1868. **Larrikins** were once regarded as hooligans or louts, but now they are often viewed with the affection that Australians have for those who 'beat the system'.

Mate

Mate has special significance in Australian English, capturing the Australian values of comradeship and equality. A **mate** is a close friend, and **mateship** is the bond between close friends. **Mate** is a form of address — 'g'day mate' — implying equality and goodwill, although it can also be used to bring someone into line — 'just watch it, mate!'

Mozzie

A mosquito. **Mozzie**, first recorded in 1936, illustrates a distinctive feature of Australian English — the addition of **-ie** or **-y** to abbreviated words or phrases. Other examples include: **barbie** 'barbecue', **blowie** 'blowfly', **Chrissy prezzie** 'Christmas present', **cossie** 'swimming costume', **sickie** 'a day's sick leave', **budgie** 'budgerigar', **lippy** 'lipstick', **maggie** 'magpie', **U-ey** 'U-turn', and **sunnies** 'sunglasses'.

Noah

A shark. This is an example of rhyming slang. In rhyming slang, an everyday word is replaced by a phrase, the last element of which rhymes with the everyday word. Thus **Captain Cook** is rhyming slang for 'a look'. Sometimes the rhyming element is omitted. Noah was originally **Noah's Ark**. Similarly, **on one's Pat** is short for **on one's Pat Malone**, 'alone'.

Ocker

A rough and uncultivated Australian. **Ocker** was recorded from 1916 as a nickname for anyone called 'Oscar', but the **ocker** as an Australian stereotype did not appear until much later. It was influenced by a television character named Ocker in the satirical 1960s comedy 'The Mavis Bramston Show'. This **Ocker** was was first recorded in 1971.

Plonk

Cheap or poor-quality wine, although Australian beer drinkers call any kind of wine **plonk**. This word had its origin with Australian soldiers in the First World War. They pronounced the French **vin blanc**, 'white wine', **van blonk**, and further transformed it into **plonk**. The Australian word has now spread to other varieties of English.

Pobblebonk

A large burrowing Australian frog. The male has a loud single-note call that sounds like **bonk**. A number of frogs calling together produce a sound like **pobblebonk**, so the frog's name comes from the sound it makes. The sound resembles the plucking of a banjo, and for this reason the frog is also called the **banjo frog**. The term **pobblebonk** was first recorded in 1965.

Pom

A British person. Also pommy. First recorded in 1912, the term was originally applied to an immigrant from Britain, and was formed by rhyming slang. A British immigrant was called a pommygrant, from the red fruit pomegranate, perhaps referring to the complexion of the new arrivals, which was then abbreviated to pommy and pom. Although some argue otherwise, it is not an acronym of prisoner of mother England.

Rort

A fraudulent or dishonest act or practice — 'a tax rort'. Also used as a verb — 'to rort the system'. **Rort** comes from the Standard English **rorty**, meaning 'boisterous, jolly', and, in the late nineteenth century, 'coarse, of dubious propriety'. The second sense of **rorty** disappeared, but has been retained in the Australian **rort**, which was first recorded in 1919

Sheila

A girl or girlfriend, a woman. This word first appeared in Australian English in 1832 with the spelling **shelah**. Both **sheila** and **shelah** are anglicised spellings of the Irish Gaelic **Síle**, and it was probably the large number of Irish migrants to Australia that led to this common Irish name becoming a general term for a 'woman'.

She'll be right

'Everything will be all right; don't worry about it.' The use of the pronoun she is common in Australian speech in phrases where the pronoun **it** is standard in other varieties of English. Other phrases such as **she's apples** and **she's sweet** indicate the same sense of 'all is going well'.

Snag

A sausage. In Australia and elsewhere **snag** has a number of meanings, including 'a submerged tree stump', 'an unexpected drawback', and more recently a 'sensitive new age guy'. But in Australia a **snag** is also a 'sausage', a sense that probably comes from the British dialect word **snag**, 'a morsel, a light meal'.

Two-up

A gambling game. Two coins are tossed in the air and bets placed on a showing of two heads or two tails. The two coins are placed tails up on a flat board called the **kip**. The **ringkeeper**, the person in charge of the **two-up ring**, calls 'come in spinner', and the **spinner** tosses the coins. It was first recorded in 1854.

Waltzing Matilda

AB Paterson's 1895 poem '**Waltzing Matilda**', sung to the tune of an old Scottish ballad, has achieved the status of unofficial national anthem. The term **walking Matilda** was first used by poet Henry Lawson in 1893. Both the **waltz** and **matilda** are probably from the German: *walzen* 'to rove, travel' and **matilda** the name travelling German apprentices gave to the knapsack in which they carried their belongings.

Woop Woop

Any remote country town or district that is supposed to be backward. The doubling of **Woop** is like the Aboriginal placename **Wagga Wagga**. The name **Bullamakanka** is used in the same way for an imaginary remote and backward place. Even more remote is the area **beyond the black stump**. **Woop Woop** was first recorded in 1918.

Wowser

A puritanical killjoy, a person who tries to force his or her narrow morality on society. Some argue that the word comes from the initial letters of the slogan **We only want social evils righted**. Its real origin is probably the British dialect word wow 'to whine, grumble, complain'. It was first recorded in 1899.

The National Museum of Australia

The National Museum of Australia tells the stories of people, events and issues that have shaped and influenced our nation. As well as using artefacts as the focus of its stories and exhibitions, the Museum utilises cutting-edge communication technologies. The core exhibitions found within the Museum are:

- Tangled Destinies: Land and People in Australia

- Nation: Symbols of Australia

- Eternity: Stories from the Emotional Heart of Australia

- Horizons: The Peopling of Australia since 1788

- First Australians: Gallery of Aboriginal and Torres Strait Islander Peoples.

About the cartoonist

David Pope is a Canberra-based freelance cartoonist best known for the political cartoons he draws for the alternative press in Australia. He is the author of three books of cartoons: *The Fish John West Reject* (1995), *Australia Incorporated* (1997), and *Hinzebrand: political cartoons in brine* (2000). His award-winning work makes regular appearances in the National Museum of Australia's annual exhibition of political humour, *Bringing the House Down*. He also draws illustrations for the *Canberra Times*.

You can visit David on the world wide web at www.scratch.com.au